Celestial Signals

In the sky, they blink and beep,
Radio waves, they giggle deep.
Starry jests through cosmic haze,
Sending laughs in goofy ways.

Aliens tune in just for fun,
Dancing satellites, one by one.
Gravity pulling on their stance,
While asteroids join in the dance.

Phasing Light

Flashing lights from distant lands,
Quasars giggle, take a stance.
Phased in rhythm, what a ride,
Jokes in waves, they surely hide.

Flickering fast, like fireflies,
Stellar chuckles fill the skies.
Bopping beats of cosmic cheer,
Making stargazers laugh and jeer.

Notes from the Nebula

Whispers float through cosmic air,
Notes of humor everywhere.
Clouds of gas, a comic show,
Poking fun at stars below.

Gassy giggles, sparkly smiles,
Stellar jokes that travel miles.
Nebulae with punchlines grand,
Wrap the cosmos hand in hand.

Pulsing Patterns in the Dark

Patterns pulse in back and forth,
Comets snicker, what a worth!
Winks and nods from outer space,
Lighthearted laughs leave no trace.

Darkness sparkles with delight,
Starry pranks on cosmic night.
In the void, a twinkling joke,
Laughter stirs from stellar smoke.

Stellar Heartbeats

In the vast expanse a star does dance,
With a wobbly spin, it's wearing its pants!
Tick-tock it giggles in jovial cheer,
While aliens wonder, 'Is that a deer?'

A pulsar spins round, it's quite the sight,
It's got better moves than most on a night!
Twinkling and chirping a cosmic tune,
The cosmos might spark, 'Is that a cartoon?'

Cosmic Chimes

In the sky's big clock, it's ticking loud,
Stars clink like glasses, oh what a crowd!
They laugh and jingle in cosmic play,
Making music that brightens the day.

A neutron star leaps, oh what a show!
With a wink and a nod, 'Look at me glow!'
When it spins just right, a merry sound,
Even black holes join, all whirl around!

Radiant Timekeepers

With each pulse, a wink, the universe beams,
Time jumps like frogs in delightful dreams.
'Hey, watch me flip!' the starlights yell,
As if they're saying, 'Isn't this swell?'

Jovial knick-knacks in the cosmic tide,
Keep ticking along in their glittery ride.
Stars steal the show with a twinkling gig,
While planets all join in, doing a jig!

The Celestial Symphony

In the grand space hall, the orchestra plays,
Comets are flutes in a dazzling display.
With supernova drums that go boom,
Little moons tap dance while bright stars zoom.

Every note is a wink, every chord a cheer,
Cosmic laugh tracks fill the velvet sphere.
Galaxies swirl as they take their cue,
Singing of nonsense, of me and of you!

Celestial Frequencies

In the cosmos, signals dance,
Little lights that take a chance.
They beep and boop, all out of tune,
Making waves like a silly cartoon.

Distant stars with their quirks and charms,
Sending us love through radio arms.
They whisper sweet nothings in Hertz so bright,
As we chuckle at their cosmic delight.

Pulsing in the Night Sky

Up in the night, a pulse goes 'beep',
A cosmic rhythm that won't let you sleep.
Like a disco ball that's just a tad shy,
Twinkling so strange, making us sigh.

Is that a star or a radio prank?
A galactic raffle we simply can't thank!
Dancing particles, a humorous crew,
Making jokes in frequencies, just for you.

Patterns of Distant Beacons

Patterns emerge on the galactic screen,
Beacons of humor, oh so serene.
They laugh in pulses, 'Look at us spin!'
While planets below just laugh and grin.

Each flicker tells a cosmic tale,
Of a star that used to drink too much ale.
They, spin and wobble, like a jolly band,
Bringing smiles to all in this vast land.

Symphony of the Night Sky

A symphony plays in the dark, oh so bright,
With drums made of stardust, what a sight!
Each note a pulse, a giggle from far,
Making tiny Earthlings wish on a star.

The music of space is a curious blend,
Where light years apart is your cosmic friend.
They serenade us with a pulsar's tune,
As we laugh along under the yawning moon.

Whispering Stars

In the night, they giggle bright,
Twinkling jokes, with sheer delight.
They wink at us, a cosmic glee,
As if they know our secrets, free.

Far away, they dance and play,
Making wishes come out to stay.
Their chatter echoes through the void,
A sparkling band, never annoyed.

Oh, those dots of fire above,
Whispers of laughter and of love.
A cosmic prattle, back and forth,
Shining humor, a galactic worth.

So when you gaze at skies so vast,
Remember, joy in light is cast.
A chorus loud, though silent, true,
The stars just dream and poke at you.

Heartbeat of the Universe

In the dark, a thump, a bump,
Cosmic rhythms make us jump.
Each pulse a chuckle, loud and clear,
The universe sings, can you hear?

Planets tap in time with glee,
A funky beat, come dance with me!
Galaxies swirl in wild delight,
Whirling laughter, a joyous flight.

Stars, they nod to this great tune,
With solar flares that dance like a balloon.
A cosmic jam session, far and wide,
Jokes and jests in the great night slide.

So listen close, feel the fun,
In every beat, we're not the only one.
A heart that throbs through space and time,
Tickling us all with a rhythm so prime.

Lighthouses in Space

Oh, distant beacons, shining bright,
Guiding lost sailors through the night.
With every flash, a wink, a cheer,
A cosmic lighthouse, never fear!

They say, 'Hey there, don't you fret,
We'll help you find your best sunset!'
With beams of laughter, shining wide,
Celestial rulers of the starry tide.

Flickers like a playful tease,
In the vastness, we feel at ease.
Every light a quirky wave,
A little chuckle from the brave.

So let the lighthouses shine their fun,
As we drift through night, on we run.
In spacetime's dance, we find our way,
Among these jests that twinkle and play.

Pulsing Light

Twinkle, twinkle, little light,
Pulsing patterns, what a sight!
Like a heart that skips and hops,
A cosmic giggle that never stops.

Each flash a joke, a playful hue,
A glimmer here, a wink at you.
It sends a message, laugh out loud,
In the stellar sea, we feel so proud.

Rhythmic beams that bounce and glide,
Tracing paths where laughter hides.
They dance across the endless space,
Creating joy, leaving a trace.

So when you gaze at skies so deep,
Remember laughter that's theirs to keep.
With every pulse, the fun ignites,
A world of whimsy, in cosmic lights.

Cosmic Lanterns in the Void

In the dark, they twist and shout,
Little lights that spin about.
Like disco balls in space so bright,
They dance and twirl, what a sight!

With a sparkle here and a pulse there,
They make the stars seem quite rare.
A cosmic party, oh so grand,
Who knew they'd take the dance floor stand?

Aliens peek through their glass,
Thinking, "What a wild brass!"
These lanterns play their funky tune,
In the shadowy dance of the moon.

So grab a drink, join the mix,
Count the beats, learn some tricks.
With rhythm in the galaxy wide,
Laugh out loud on this stellar ride!

Pulsing Through the Cosmos

In the void, they send a beat,
With a pulse that can't be beat.
Like funky heartbeats far and lone,
They make the cosmos dance and groan.

Oh, what a sight, these twinkling dots,
Throwing parties in their spots.
With every pulse, a joke they tell,
Stars all around can't help but yell!

"Why did the star join the race?"
"To find a friend in a greater space!"
They giggle and twinkle with such delight,
As they chirp through the cosmic night.

So come and join the stellar fun,
Under the light of the distant sun.
No RSVP needed, just bring your cheer,
The universe party is finally here!

Radiance in the Void

In the silence of the night,
Radiance gives us quite a fright!
A flash, a boom, then it's done,
Just playful sparks on the run.

"Is that a star or just a prank?"
"Just wait, it's cooling in the tank!"
Giggles echo in the black,
Oh, the laughter they unpack!

Pulsating rhythms, all around,
A cosmic circus can be found.
With each bright flash, a silly jig,
Space disco, welcome to the gig!

They twirl in rhythm, they leap and twine,
A cosmic dance, it's simply divine.
When you think it's serious and neat,
Remember, the stars love a good beat!

Signals from Beyond

Signals zipping through the sky,
A cosmic text, oh my, oh my!
"Did you see that tweet from Mars?"
"No, I was counting all the stars!"

They beep and boop with fancy style,
Making scientists scratch their dial.
"Are they chatting or just having fun?"
When signals play, a game's begun!

"They invite us to their cosmic fair?"
"I'll bring a cake, we'll rock the air!"
Their humor travels at the speed of light,
With cosmic grins, oh what a sight!

So when you tune into their sign,
Remember, laughter transcends time.
With whispers of fun from afar,
The universe is quite the star!

Celestial Conversations

In the silence of space, they chat and they giggle,
Stars swap their jokes, and planets just wiggle.
Neutron stars wink, with a pulse in their might,
Cosmic comedians, shining so bright.

Asteroids tumble, a clumsy ballet,
While comets just laugh, all the way they sway.
Galaxies spin tales, with a flicker and glow,
Creating a chuckle, that dances below.

Rhapsody of Radiance

In every flicker, a ticklish jest,
A burst of laughter, from light-years that's pressed.
Supernovae chuckle with a bang and a flair,
While photons play tag in the cool cosmic air.

Waves of giggles ripple through cosmic sea,
As black holes pretend to be just like a bee.
They buzz round and round in their spiral delight,
Making fun of the guests at the dance of the night.

Frequency of Forever

Chirps from a pulsar, a quirky little tune,
Echoing lightly through the celestial dune.
With rhythms that tickle the fabric of time,
These cosmic DJs, spinning beats so sublime.

Their frequencies jostle, with humor and cheer,
Sending out laughs that only stars hear.
Jovial cadences bounce off of each sphere,
As each twinkling star has a joke to endear.

Sonic Starlight

Underneath starlight, the cosmos does play,
With sounds full of mischief, in an astral ballet.
Pulses of rhythm make comets go zoom,
While black holes just chuckle, consuming the gloom.

As waves of delight twirl through vastness of space,
The universe grins, at a cosmic embrace.
Whispers of laughter, in the void they resound,
In a symphony silly, where joy knows no bound.

Time's Celestial Pulse

In space where time does jest,
Stars twinkle like they're dressed,
Each blink a cosmic wink,
As clocks all stop to think.

Galaxies do their dance,
So bright, they take a chance,
A humorous ballet spun,
With laughter 'til they run.

Light years have become a jest,
Time spent is surely blessed,
In this cosmic comedy,
Who needs a grand decree?

With echoes of the past,
Each snap and crackle casts,
A tick-tock, rib-tickling
In waves that keep on giggling.

Celestial Rhythms of the Night

In the dark where starlight plays,
Galaxies hold sway for days,
While comets race with glee,
Shining bright, oh can you see?

Neutron stars spin and sway,
Doing their waltz in a cosmic ballet,
Their glowing hearts go tick-tock,
Making a splash like a big block rock.

From craters to the moons so sly,
It's a cosmic joke, oh my oh my,
As asteroids chuckle, twinkle and shine,
They mime a scene from a grand design.

Orbits twist like roller coasters,
In this sky of giggling roasters,
Where even the black holes grin,
A universe full of quirky spin.

Signals of the Silenced

In the void where silence reigns,
Waves of laughter break the chains,
Pulses echo, a cosmic chime,
In a lull that seems to rhyme.

The stars giggle in their sleep,
While comets take a cosmic leap,
As satellites spin tales untold,
In radio waves of shimmer and gold.

Like playful children on a spree,
They bounce around, oh can't you see?
Each signal's just a silly tease,
A cosmic game that aims to please.

So tune in to the cosmic jokes,
Because even space likes a couple pokes,
In this vastness, humor's found,
We're all just stardust dancing 'round.

Cosmic Pulsations

In the expanse where laughter reigns,
Stars burst forth like grains in chains,
Pulsations bounce from here to there,
Each one whispering, "Who's in the air?"

Neutron hearts beat wild and free,
A cosmic rhythm for you and me,
On a drum of space, they tap and dance,
Holding a universe in a playful trance.

Light-speed banter makes time warp,
Galactic giggles, a lively sport,
With each tick, they frolic and spin,
Chasing shadows with a cheeky grin.

So join the cosmic raucous show,
Where signals play and photons flow,
The stars wink at us from their heights,
In a stellar frolic filled with delights.

Stellar Resonance

In the night sky, they blink and twirl,
Like disco balls in a space-age swirl,
They send out signals, oh what a tease,
I bet they gossip on cosmic breeze.

They laugh at stars, the jokes are bright,
A few light-years travel, quite a sight,
With every pulse, they tickle our brains,
A dance of quarks in electric chains.

When they spin, they say, 'Look at us go!'
Like ballet dancers moving slow,
Yet here we are, just gazing in awe,
I think I saw one flossing its jaw.

So next time you gaze at the night's grand show,
Imagine them winking, putting on a show,
In this cosmic club, they're the life of the screen,
Just pulses and giggles, living the dream.

Whispers in the Stellar Wind

From far-off realms, the whispers ride,
Through cosmic canyons, oh so wide,
'They're in a rush!' the starlight shouts,
Echoing musings, without a doubt.

With every pulse, a secret friend,
Tales of the cosmos they duly send,
'Hey, what's the matter?' they seem to say,
'Just searching for laughs as I bounce away!'

They tickle light years with a gentle touch,
Creating riddles that mean so much,
In the void, they crack a cosmic joke,
And giggles flutter like stardust smoke.

So listen closely, for they never tire,
Their echoes sing like a celestial choir,
In the stellar wind, their laughter sways,
A cosmic comedy that never decays.

Celestial Loops

Loops in the sky, round and round,
They spin and shimmer, making sounds,
'They're very busy!' we often cry,
As they orbit joyfully in the sky.

These rhythmic bursts are quite the show,
Like cosmic hula hoops, watch them go,
With every turn, they giggle and play,
'We're the fun ones! What else can we say?'

In their waltz, they wink and beam,
Flashing like stars in a cartoon dream,
They trade silly dances across the night,
Making space travel a true delight.

So join the fun, don't miss your cue,
Looping with laughter till we feel brand new,
For in this grand stage of the starry pairs,
Every pulse is a joke that joyfully flares.

Orbiting Melodies

In endless circles, the tunes arise,
As oscillations adorn the skies,
Each rhythm pulses like a human heart,
A symphony crafted, a cosmic art.

They spin and sway, a galactic orchestra,
Serenading planets, a whimsical panorama,
'This beat is groovy!' they quip with glee,
As they strum the notes of the galaxy.

With every wave, a chuckle unfurls,
Tickling stardust, like ribbons and pearls,
Dancing through space with a wink and a tumble,
A melody of laughter that makes us all fumble.

So turn up the dial, let the starlight sway,
Join in the chorus of night and day,
For in this cosmic play of notes and chords,
We find our smiles, reaching for the stars.

Echoes of Celestial Time

In the sky where stars do twine,
A beacon winks, it's out of line.
Twirling on a cosmic spin,
Those rhythmic lights, they're in for a grin.

Tick tock, they dance with flair,
Sending signals through the air.
Count the beats, they make us laugh,
Are they friends, or just a gaffe?

Bright pulsars play a silly game,
Flashing bright to earn their fame.
Tickle your mind, they keep it fun,
Who knew stars joke when day is done?

So look up at night's grand show,
With twinkling lights that ebb and flow.
They're just stars with humor so bright,
Creating joy in the velvet night.

A Symphony of Pulses

In cosmic halls where silence reigns,
Funky beats defy the chains.
Bump and grind, they throb and thrash,
A stellar concert, quite the splash!

Tickles of light, a rolling beat,
Bopping along with cosmic heat.
Pulsars groove, the universe claps,
Spinning bright in their funky caps.

A big band of the night sky,
Even comets can't deny.
They strut and sway with flair and zest,
These twinkling stars are truly blessed!

So let's join in this cosmic jam,
Boogie with a starlit slam.
In the vastness, we find our chance,
To waltz and twirl in a stellar dance!

The Song of Distant Stars

Distant stars with voices bright,
Sing a tune that feels just right.
Humming soft across the void,
A melody that can't be destroyed.

They strum the strings of time and space,
With cosmic humor, they embrace.
Winking down, a playful tease,
Can you hear the giggles on the breeze?

A chorus made of light and cheer,
Tickling the vastness, far and near.
With each pulse, they rhyme and play,
Casting shadows on a sunny day.

Join the song, let laughter soar,
As starry jesters evermore.
In the cosmic choir we belong,
Swaying to the universe's song!

Galactic Rhythms

Round and round, a cosmic race,
Stars are laughing in their place.
Galaxies swirl with a twist,
A pulse of joy you can't resist.

Beneath the veil of night and dreams,
Beacons shine with glittering beams.
They drum and dance, it's quite a sight,
Galactic rhythms taking flight.

Join the fun, just gaze above,
Unlock the secrets, feel the love.
Each pulse whispers a little jest,
Reminding us we're all so blessed.

So spin along with the stars so bright,
In this cosmic dance, take flight.
For in the laughter of space and time,
We find our beats, our quirky rhyme.

Celestial Echo Chamber

Bouncing waves through space, they sing,
A stellar choir with a cosmic zing.
They dance in rhythm, twirl and spin,
Making spacetime giggle, oh what a win!

Signals zipping like fireflies at night,
Whispers of atoms in a playful flight.
Waves collide and ricochet in cheer,
Echoes of stars that we all can hear!

Galactic jesters with a twinkling grin,
Throwing a fiesta as lightwaves begin.
In this chamber of echoes, laughter's the key,
Join in the fun; it's a cosmic jamboree!

So grab a friend, put on your space shoes,
For a laugh with the cosmos, you cannot lose.
With beats that are catchy and moves that are neat,
These radiant pulsars can't be beat!

Cosmic Pulsations

Tick-tock, tick-tock, the universe plays,
Pulses arriving in rhythmic arrays.
A cosmic dance, a stellar tease,
Wobbling around with wondrous ease.

They hop and skip, making the stars laugh,
Radiating joy like a cosmic giraffe.
Bouncing around like a party balloon,
Who knew the universe could be so in tune?

With every pulse, a chuckle ignites,
Galaxies laughing in shimmering lights.
A beat that's contagious, electric, alive,
In this cosmic party, we all will thrive!

So hold on tight to your celestial hat,
As these cosmic rhythms make us all chat.
Pulsations of giggles, joy flies in space,
Dancing with laughter in the vast, open place!

Luminous Time Travelers

Bouncing through ages in a shining spree,
Time travelers dressed in bright energy.
With every flicker, they steal your breath,
Teaching us laughter amidst cosmic death.

They skip through epochs, twinkling with glee,
Who knew light could possess such esprit?
With each pulse, they whisper tales so bold,
Of yesteryears packed in glittering gold.

They tap dance on photons, it's quite the show,
Wobbling into the future, fast and slow.
Come join the fun in this luminous race,
With time on our side, let's laugh in space!

A journey so silly, we giggle and jive,
As these travelers shine—oh, they make us thrive!
With histories funny and stories so rich,
In the vastness of time, find a cosmic niche!

Ethereal Call from the Cosmos

Wave hello to the void, a silly shout,
Echoes of laughter that swirl and sprout.
A call from beyond, can you hear the cheer?
Galaxies chuckling as they pull you near.

Through starlit corridors, hear the delight,
Waves of giggles shooting through the night.
With every beam, we get a tease,
The universe's humor isn't hard to seize!

Imagine the stars playing peek-a-boo,
With glimmers and shimmers, oh so true.
As comets waltz in this earthly dance,
Even black holes can't resist the chance.

So heed the call from the celestial spread,
Join in the fun where no one dreads.
With laughter ringing through the cosmic hall,
We're all together, answering the call!

Timeless Echoes

In the void where they spin so fast,
Whispers of light from the distant past.
Beaming their tales from afar,
Sending us giggles in a cosmic jar.

Round and round, they never get tired,
While we down here get easily wired.
Counting their beats with a funny face,
They laugh at our rush, keeping their pace.

Each pulse a wink that they fashion,
As they twirl in a humorous passion.
Floating through space, they share a joke,
With all of us, they softly poke.

So next time you gaze into the night,
Remember their fun in the endless flight.
Timeless echoes in the grand design,
It's merely a cosmic punchline divine!

Cosmic Metronome

Tick-tock of the universe, what a sight,
Stars playing music in the dead of night.
With every pulse, they tap their feet,
Swinging through space, keeping it neat.

What do you call a star with a plan?
A metronome, or just a fun fan?
Bouncing and beeping, they never tire,
Setting the stage for a dance so higher.

Quantized chaos in a rhythm divine,
Cosmic giggles keep us all in line.
As they pulsate, we can't help but sway,
To the beat of the universe's quirky play.

So let's clap our hands and give a cheer,
For the cosmic drummer that we hold dear.
In every shadow, in every foam,
We find the humor in their vast tome.

Dance of the Celestial Beacons

In the dance of lights, they twirl and spin,
Cosmic stars invite us to join in.
With a wink and a nod, they shake the night,
A cosmic disco, what a sight!

Galactic beams in a playful race,
Sending signals to a far-off place.
Each pulse a pirouette, a shimmy so fun,
Who knew the cosmos could host everyone?

Jiving and jiggling across the void,
It's a party in space, we should avoid!
But if we could join, oh what a blast,
Dancing with beacons, forget the past!

So throw on your sparkles, let's make a scene,
In the celestial ballroom, bright and serene.
With laughter and joy, we'll light up the night,
As the cosmos twirls in infinite delight!

Sonic Waves of the Cosmos

In waves so groovy, they surf the night,
Whistling tunes of astonishing light.
Sonic vibrations in the void so grand,
With alien rhythms that no one planned.

A cosmic DJ spins the stellar sound,
Beaming beats that echo around.
Every pulse is a note, every spin a catch,
Sending us music that we can't match.

Riding the wavelengths, they laugh and play,
Who knew starlight could swing this way?
So we'll dance along to their quirky tunes,
Beneath the watchful gaze of the moon.

In this cosmic concert, we sway and cheer,
Abundant joy echoes near and dear.
For all the laughter in the wave's embrace,
Let's join the fun in this vast, wild space!

Harmonics of Space

In a galaxy far from here,
Stars tap dance without fear.
They shimmy and shake to cosmic beats,
While black holes enjoy the treats.

Neutron stars do a funky spin,
As quasars grin with a cheeky grin.
With each pulse, they play a tune,
Making the space-time quite a boon.

Light waves wobble, it's a show,
Gravity joins, putting on a flow.
Asteroids tap with rocks so bold,
Simmering stories waiting to be told.

Galactic giggles echo through night,
While meteors impress with their flight.
The cosmos hums a joyous note,
As stellar parties freely float.

Light's Intervals

The light takes breaks in between beams,
Like owls taking naps in their dreams.
A twinkle here, a flicker there,
Photons love to play, I swear!

Waves crash in a cosmic laugh,
Each interval a funny staff.
Shooting stars wink with delight,
As light races at hyper speed night.

When photons stop to share a joke,
You can hear the universe choke.
Bright ideas burst with glee,
While darkness groans, 'Oh let me be!'

Time borrows giggles from light's parade,
Rendering moments, not afraid.
In a twist of space, they find their fun,
A dance of photons, never done.

Cosmic Heartstrings

In the void, chords strum with flair,
Stars sing sweetly, spinning in air.
With each pulse, a rhythm flows,
Universes dance, as everyone knows.

Gravity pulls at elastic hearts,
While comets swirl, and take their parts.
Cosmic choirs belt out their tunes,
Serenading planets under moons.

A pulsar's beat is a jolly laugh,
As galaxies join in the craft.
They mingle and jive to the spacerock beat,
Creating a symphony, oh so sweet!

Twirling through the starlit night,
Strumming on those heartstrings, what a sight!
With cosmic whispers and radiant gleams,
In the grand ballet, nothing's as it seems.

Universe in Symmetry

In a world where quarks play fair,
They dance in pairs, quite a rare affair.
Symmetrical twirls, oh what a sight,
Even photons can't resist the light!

Planets align in a cosmic line,
Funny fates twist in perfect design.
Black holes chuckle, 'Here comes the fun!'
While asteroids aim their shots like a gun.

Even the elements join the spree,
Carbon and helium, sipping tea.
With laughter they forge in unity,
Crafting life's quirks, such a community!

In stellar patterns, they find their groove,
As each little quirk gives space its move.
Twirling and swirling, just take a peek,
In the grand symmetry, life plays hide and seek.

Starlight Symphony

In the sky, a dance so bright,
Stars twirl like they're high as a kite.
Beams flash out just like a wink,
Making us laugh, thinking, 'What do they drink?'

With each pulse, the cosmos sings,
Wobbly beats, like quirky strings.
A cosmic show, a wild parade,
While space squirrels throw confetti made!

Galaxies groove to quirky tunes,
As Saturn spins, it makes us swoon.
With every twirl, the stardust flies,
And space-time tickles, oh how it pries!

Neutron stars beat like a drum,
The universe hums, 'Aren't we fun?'
In this vast expanse, we dance about,
While aliens join in, no doubt!

Cosmic Cadence

A rhythm found, a funky beat,
In the void where starlings meet.
Planets stomp and asteroids sway,
In the cosmic cabaret, hip-hip-hooray!

Light years away, the laughter flows,
As black holes giggle, no one knows.
Meteor showers throw a party blast,
And planets spin, oh, so fast!

Orbiting moons bring their own jams,
With Saturn's rings, they twirl like hams.
Dancing stars with twinkling flair,
Whispering secrets to folks up there!

The cosmos chuckles, a joyful ride,
In celestial swings, we take stride.
So let's join this madcap cheer,
As starlight winks and draws us near!

The Universe's Metronome

Tick-tock, the stars align,
A cosmic dance to sip our wine.
The universe plays its silly song,
As we sway and bounce along!

Pulses echo through the night,
Making wishes feel just right.
A starlit joke, a wink, a grin,
As waves of laughter draw us in!

Galaxies spin in a dizzy rush,
While comets play with a colorful brush.
A metronome of fun and cheer,
In dreamy realms where time's unclear!

With each beat, the cosmos beams,
We frolic in our silly dreams.
Every pulse a giggle in space,
Where funny moments find their place!

Pulses Beneath the Night Sky

Under stars that wink and glow,
The night hums a tune we know.
With pulses bright, we dance and play,
As cosmic critters join the fray!

Galactic friends in rhythmic glee,
Moonbeams join the jamboree.
Stars giggle as they drift on by,
Pulses twirling, oh me, oh my!

Neutron beats go thump and thud,
In this heavenly, starry flood.
Each pulse a tickle, a playful tease,
Making wishes ride on a cosmic breeze!

So raise a glass, toast to the night,
With laughter and joy, oh what a sight!
Beneath the sky, we join the fun,
In this quasar party, we've just begun!

The Pulse of Infinity

In the vast expanse, things spin and twirl,
A light show unfolds, like a cosmic whirl.
Neutron stars dance, with a wink and a nod,
Tick-tocking in space—my, how they prod!

With pulse beats so steady, they've got style,
Sending signals like they're playing a dial.
Synchronized rhythms that make us all grin,
Is it a message, or just a light spin?

They pulse with a flair, oh what a delight,
Winking from corners of the endless night.
With a laugh and a beam, they whisper and tease,
Dancing on waves of the stellar breeze.

So raise up a glass to their radiant game,
In this quirky cosmos, we're all quite the same.
Though light-years divide, we're tethered by fun,
Intergalactic friends, shining on the run!

Light's Dance Across the Void

In the cosmic ballet, a twinkle turns bright,
Stars doing the cha-cha, oh what a sight!
Waltzing through darkness, they shake and they jive,
Sending out flashes, oh how they strive!

Every tick of a star, a beat in the night,
Spinning like dancers, just out of our sight.
With sparkles and grins, they light up the dark,
Making us giggle with each little spark!

Throw a cosmic party, let's twirl to the sound,
Of pulsars and novas that play all around.
A rhythm of laughter fills up the great space,
As we join in the fun, all ready to race!

So laugh with the stars in their shimmering glow,
For light that can tickle is all that we know.
A cosmic parade of delight on display,
Let's dance through the night, come what may!

Cosmic Harmonium

In the grand cosmic hall, where echoes abound,
Pulsars are tuning, oh what a sound!
With keys made of starlight, they play a fine tune,
Harmonies drift beneath the silvery moon.

They pluck at our hearts, with each beat they send,
A comical song that will never quite end.
With giggles of gravity, they tickle the void,
In the orchestra's glow, we are all overjoyed.

Each pulse a note in this stellar charade,
Creating a symphony none can evade.
So dance in the stardust, feel free to sway,
As the galaxies play on, come join in the fray!

Through filters of laughter, we watch and we cheer,
For each little pulse brings the cosmos so near.
In this cosmic concert, we all play a part,
Echoing laughter from the depths of our heart!

Stellar Soundscapes

In the celestial park, where the echoes are loud,
Stars strum their guitars, oh aren't they proud?
They riff through the dark, with a twist and a spin,
Creating a melody that makes the light grin.

With beams like a bow, they serenade time,
Pulsating with joy, what a rhythm sublime!
They giggle like children, shining in play,
In a universe grand, making light of the day.

Each twinkle a note, in this vast cosmic jam,
They tease and they tangle, oh how they slam!
With laughter and joy, they dance to the beat,
In the stellar soundscapes, oh isn't it sweet?

So let's join the chorus, and sing along too,
With pulsars and stars, let your spirit break through.
In the grand cosmic show, there's no need to frown,
For laughter's the ticket to wear your crown!

Stars that Sing

In a galaxy far to our right,
The stars are jamming, what a sight!
They play a tune, so pure and bright,
But one sings flat, and we take flight.

In the cosmic bar, they're a band of old,
Strumming their beams, bright and bold.
It's a jam session, never controlled,
With a chorus of jokes, that never gets cold.

The nebula giggles, a soft giggling sound,
While planets are dancing, spinning around.
The comets are twirling, all unbound,
In this stellar concert, pure joy is found.

But watch out for black holes, they might steal the show,
Sucking up notes, leaving just woe.
Yet here in the cosmos, laughter will glow,
For every lost tune, a new one will grow.

Chasing the Light's Pulse

Chasing the light, on a wild spree,
Racing through space, oh so carefree!
We play tag with photons, come join me,
Twinkling stars whisper, "You can't catch me!"

In this game of light, we tumble and spin,
Giggles echo where the fun will begin.
Galaxies wink, with a cheeky grin,
While dark matter lurks, trying to win.

Stopping for snacks, a cosmic delight,
We munch on stardust, oh what a sight!
But watch out for meteors, they might take flight,
And ruin our picnic, with a flash of light!

Finally, we rest, on a comet so grand,
Giggling together, hand in hand.
In this game of chasing, isn't it planned?
That laughter resounds in our space-faring band.

Celestial Rhythm

Bouncing in time, with a cosmic beat,
Stars do the dance, isn't it neat?
Loops and twirls, can't feel my feet,
As planets join in, what a treat!

Dancing on neutron, a wild affair,
They spin to the rhythm, without a care.
Shooting stars leap, in the cold air,
While black holes quietly plot, as they stare.

But don't lose your step, or you'll end up lost,
In the swirling chaos, what a cost!
The universe chuckles, it's their frost,
While the sun winks, giving us toast.

So keep up the groove, it's a cosmic show,
The rhythm of space, it will always flow.
With laughter and joy in the stars' afterglow,
Let's dance with the light, let our spirits grow.

Echoes in the Cosmic Void

In the cosmic void, echoes ring,
A bizarre choir, what could they bring?
Singing in laughter, while comets swing,
They dance to the tunes that the cosmos fling!

One echo says, "Do you hear that roar?"
It's just a black hole, looking for more.
With a laugh, we dodge and explore,
Finding new echoes on this vast shore.

With every bounce, we chuckle and cheer,
The void isn't empty, it whispers so near.
Each sound tells a story, crystal clear,
Spreading joy through the cosmos, oh dear!

So join in the fun, let's play our part,
In the echoing cosmos, let's take heart.
For in this void, laughter is an art,
As we spin in the dark, a luminous start.

Harmonies of Distant Worlds

In the cosmos, weird sounds play,
Neutron stars dancing away.
Like a cosmic DJ's wild mix,
Jiving in his spacey tricks.

Waves of giggles bounce and swirl,
Through the universe's twirly whirl.
With beats that tickle and delight,
Stars wobble in the dark of night.

Lights that flash with quirky flair,
Twinkling in a cosmic pair.
Who knew that stars could really groove?
In this void, they truly prove.

So if you hear a funny beep,
It's just some stars lost in their leap.
Join the laughter, keep it bright,
In this crazy cosmic night.

Celestial Beats

Listen close to the cosmic song,
Beats from afar, they're never wrong.
Rhythmic thumps from the great unknown,
Spinning light tunes from a shining throne.

Bouncing beams that tickle the ear,
As comets trail with a comet cheer.
Galactic grooves that make you sway,
In the void, it's a disco play.

Stars synchro dance, what a sight!
Who knew they'd party all night?
With quarks and leptons in the mix,
It's a space rave, full of tricks!

So if your heart skips with the beat,
Just know it's not the cosmic heat.
It's those celestial pals in glee,
Making music through eternity!

Stellar Cadences

Distant sprays of light in flight,
Composing tunes of pure delight.
Every pulse, a comic beat,
Stars bustling with their cosmic feet.

Giggles echo from afar,
As planets spin, they raise the bar.
With each twinkle and glimmer sweet,
They rock the universe to the beat.

Bright quasars crack a wink or two,
With rhythms that make the stardust stew.
Catchy hooks from a world unknown,
The galaxy's symphony has grown!

So grab your dance shoes, join the show,
In this wild space where giggles flow.
Beats from the void will keep you light,
As stars and laughter take their flight.

Rhythmic Echoes in Infinity

In the void where silly sounds roam,
Stars bounce beats like they're at home.
With every thud, a chuckle's found,
As lightyears pass, they dance around.

Whispers of laughter through the dark,
Messages sent with a goofy spark.
Each pulse a wink, a nod, a tease,
In this vastness, let's just seize!

Galaxies roll with humor so bright,
Casting their glow, oh what a sight!
Cosmic giggles float on the breeze,
Through time and space, they tease with ease.

So when you ponder life's great jest,
Remember the stars in their cosmic fest.
With rhythmic echoes, they bring delight,
In the heart of the cosmos, shining bright!

Spinning Stars and Stretching Time

In the sky, they spin and twirl,
Like cosmic dancers, giving a whirl.
Tick-tock, they joke with gravity's hold,
Making time bend; it's a sight to behold.

Flashing lights play hide and seek,
Their silent laughter, oh so chic.
Each pulse is a wink, a cheeky delight,
As they spin through the cosmos, day and night.

Who knew stars could be such a tease?
Tickling space with cosmic breeze.
They giggle as they twine and glide,
In the grand dance, there's nowhere to hide.

With a flick and a twist, they pull a prank,
Our telescopes watching, they smirk and flank.
In their radiant glow, we find our cheer,
Let's toast to these stars, full of good humor here.

Radiant Echoes

Echoes bounce in the night so bright,
A game of tag in the starlit light.
Each signal rings, a cosmic bell,
As they chuckle, casting a spell.

Like a cosmic duo with jokes to share,
Waves of laughter fill the air.
With every pulse, their humor glows,
Filling voids where no one goes.

Whispers travel across the vast dark,
Sending giggles to every spark.
A stellar punchline hangs on high,
Leaving us quizzical, oh my, oh my!

When we gaze up, our hearts take flight,
Chasing echoes, a joyful sight.
They revel in jest with a rhythmic beat,
Our cosmic jesters, oh so sweet.

Celestial Waves

Waves of laughter ripple afar,
From spinning giants, gleaming star.
In every pulse, a chuckle sneaks,
As time ticks in these galactic peaks.

With playful spins, they ride the tide,
Cosmic jokers, they chuckle with pride.
Shimmering dances light up the sky,
An interstellar laugh, oh my!

They tease the universe with beams so bright,
Playing hide and seek with our sight.
Clark and his pals, in space, they glide,
Making sure laughter's always inside.

So, let's wave back, in this cosmic joke,
With every twinkle, they nudge, they poke.
In their glowing antics, we find our glee,
Riding their waves, come play with me!

Illuminated Secrets of the Sky

Beneath their light, secrets unfold,
In whispers bright, the stars are bold.
They laugh at our joys, what a cosmic scene,
Hiding tidbits in shining sheen.

Each flicker tells tales in cosmic jest,
Poking fun while we try our best.
What tricks they play on our curious minds,
With radiant secrets, the universe binds.

With a cosmic grin, they share their fun,
Lightyears away, their mischief's begun.
These luminous jesters float in delight,
Illuminating the wonders of night.

Oh, the mischief of those twinkling eyes,
Crafting stories under starlit skies.
Join the dance, let the dreams take flight,
In the laughter of stars, everything feels right.

Whispers of the Celestial Clock

Tick-tock, the stars play,
Dancing in a cosmic ballet.
Each pulse a joke that they tell,
Echoes of laughter that dwell.

In the void where time unwinds,
Galactic giggles, oh how it binds.
With every blink, a playful tease,
Creating rhythms that aim to please.

Galaxies spin with a chuckle bright,
Flickering fast in the dark of night.
How can light be so funny too?
The cosmos laughs, and so should you!

As planets whirl in humorous haste,
Time flows by with a jovial taste.
So listen close, let your heart's beat sync,
With the universe's wink, just have a drink!

Luminescent Lullabies

In the cradle of night, stars hum and sway,
Singing glowing tunes that lead us astray.
A chorus of beams, shining so bright,
Telling silly stories of cosmic delight.

Wobbling orbs with giggles galore,
Swinging through time, demanding encore.
With every flash, a whimsical glance,
The universe chuckles in a cosmic dance.

Do you hear the laughter, the twinkling sounds?
In the fabric of space, humor abounds.
Time drips like honey, sweet and thick,
Daring us to join in the cosmic trick!

Bouncing bullets of light in their glee,
Joking about the mysteries of what will be.
These lullabies tease the sleep from our eyes,
As we drift away beneath starry skies.

Timekeepers of the Galaxy

Watch the clocks that tick and tock,
Galaxies play with time like a rock.
Jovial timers in celestial parade,
Counting laughs rather than a trade.

With every beat, a quip unfurls,
Whirling in laughter, the cosmos twirls.
How many stars does it take to beam?
Just one to start an eternal meme!

Keep up with the cosmic play,
Time's a prank, come what may.
A wink of light, a jest of fate,
In the universe's giggling state.

Watch out, black holes — they might just snort,
At the clumsy galaxies caught in their sport.
Timekeepers, pranksters of stellar delight,
With humor and light, they dance through the night!

Harmony of Quantum Lights

In the quantum realm, hilarity sings,
Particles waltzing on invisible strings.
Ticklish quarks, they bounce and play,
Joking about the laws of the day.

With flashes and twirls, they find their groove,
Fumbling through dimensions, in a smooth move.
Laughter echoes through the atom's core,
As energies giggle and settle the score.

An electron chuckles, a proton grins,
In the dance of creation, where humor begins.
How strange is the dance of time and space,
Yet wildly funny, a celestial race!

So, let's join the laughter — break out in cheer,
As quantum giggles appear far and near.
In this strange ballet of the microscopic,
The secrets of the cosmos feel delightfully comic!

Dance of the Heavenly Spheres

In the night sky, a strobe light spins,
Stars do the cha-cha, while Saturn grins.
Neptune tripped and fell, like a cosmic clown,
Jupiter's got moves, wearing a funny crown.

Asteroids slide, in tap shoes they glide,
Comets launch a conga, with a stellar pride.
Galaxies whir, in a spin class so bright,
While black holes suck dancers, right out of sight.

Meteors dash, like they're late for a date,
While Venus hula hoops, it's a celestial state.
Mercury's zippy, can't find its cue,
Yet in this grand waltz, there's always room for you.

So join the fun, in this cosmic spree,
With each twirl and flash, just float with glee.
The universe laughs, in a stellar embrace,
As we dance through the stars, in this endless space.

Frequencies of the Infinite

From afar comes a beep, is it music or noise?
With satellites jamming, oh what a poise!
A radio wave's wiggle, a raucous delight,
Spinning frequencies, like twirling at night.

Signals bounce like rubber, what a crazy sound,
While pulsars twinkle and hop all around.
Their rhythm is quirky, with hiccups and grins,
Making space-time giggle, as laughter begins.

Frequency up, frequency down,
Every beat makes the cosmos astound.
The universe winks, each laugh a tune,
Echoing wonder, beneath the bright moon.

So tune in your heart, to this cosmic song,
For the universe knows, it won't steer you wrong.
Vibrations of joy, dance through the night,
In this vast symphony, everything's bright!

Poetic Echoes of the Universe

In the darkness of space, whispers abound,
Echoes of laughter, in silence profound.
Stars yodel and murmur, in cosmic delight,
While black holes giggle, swallowing light.

Comets scream by, with a tickle and tease,
Shooting past planets, like a cosmic sneeze.
Their tails swirl around, a glittery jest,
Making meteor showers, pop with a zest.

The Milky Way chuckles, it spills its own tale,
As galaxies spin, on this grand cosmic scale.
In the quiet of night, we listen and hear,
The universe chuckling, so loud and so clear.

So gather your thoughts, let the echoes play,
Dance with the rhythm, as night turns to day.
In the poetic silence, laughter sings true,
For the universe's jokes, are written for you.

Pulsar Serenade

Oh lonely pulsar, in your spin you twirl,
Sending out rays, with a twinkly whirl.
Each beat is a wink, full of cheeky charm,
As you serenade stars with your luminous harm.

A rhythm so steady, yet playful and bright,
You're the DJ of heavens, spinning through night.
Your light pulses out, like a cosmic high-five,
Telling the universe, I'm happy, alive!

With each grand rotation, you giggle and say,
Watch out for satellites, don't get in my way!
The dance of the heavens, so funny and bold,
In your twinkling serenade, adventures unfold.

So here's to your laughter, a galactic ballet,
As you string together, the starlight display.
With every good vibe, the cosmos does cheer,
For the joyous pulsar, we all hold dear.

Resonance Across Galaxies

In the dance of cosmic rays,
Stars twinkle in bizarre ways.
A neutron star's wobbly spin,
Makes the black holes laugh and grin.

They chirp like crickets on a spree,
Creating chaos in a glee.
When they pulse, they steal the show,
Leaving us in a cosmic glow.

Galactic neighbors stop and stare,
Feeling rhythms in the air.
With every beat, a tale of fun,
As light bounces, they all run.

In the vast and endless night,
Laughing at their dizzy flight.
Oh, what joy in starry beams,
Echoes sound like silly dreams.

Celestial Melodies

In a universe so vast and wide,
Stars perform with a cosmic stride.
They swirl and spin while making sounds,
Joking with the dark that surrounds.

A pulsar sings a funny tune,
Bouncing off the silver moon.
Its beat brings giggles, what a scene,
As galaxies tease in a dance routine.

Waltzing planets join the fun,
Execution bold, around they run.
Comets tailing, join the song,
In this cosmos, nothing's wrong!

With each pulse, a laugh reverberates,
Gravity pulls, yet joy awaits.
So let's dance under stellar rays,
And celebrate these cosmic plays!

Ethereal Rhythms

A pulsar leads a cosmic band,
With beats that make the stardust stand.
Each rotation sparks a cheer,
As alien friends gather near.

In the silence, laughter bursts,
Galaxies find their playful thirsts.
They twist and turn in jovial spin,
In every wave, silly grins begin.

Asteroids play the tambourine,
While stars wink bright, oh so keen.
They keep the tempo, quite absurd,
Echoes bouncing, no one heard.

With a tick-tock, the dance goes on,
Through endless night until the dawn.
In the void, connections form,
In laughter's arms, they keep us warm.

Pulsar Arias

A star so bright, it loves to pulse,
Sings a tune that's quite repulsive.
Its rhythm makes the quasars quake,
In cosmic humor, they all partake.

Dancing light beams, a joke or two,
Galactic jesters, a charming view.
Each aria sparkles with delight,
While comets giggle, flying bright.

The universe plays its silly part,
As pulsars tickle the cosmic heart.
In every note, far and wide,
Laughter echoes, we just can't hide.

So let's sing along with grace,
In this humorous, starry space.
For among the stars that brightly shine,
The joy of laughter is truly divine.

www.ingramcontent.com/pod-product-compliance
Lightning Source LLC
Chambersburg PA
CBHW071826160426
43209CB00003B/214